GW01326319

Withdrawn For Sale

SCRAP MATERIALS

Mike Roussel

Illustrated by
Malcolm S. Walker

Withdrawn For Sale

Craft Projects

CLAY
FABRICS AND YARNS
NATURAL MATERIALS
PAPER AND CARD
SCRAP MATERIALS
WOOD

NORFOLK LIBRARY AND
INFORMATION SERVICE

SUPPLIER	B F S
INVOICE No.	1042400
ORDER DATE	2 0 MAR 1990
COPY. No.	

J 745.5

© Copyright 1989 Wayland (Publishers) Ltd.

First published in 1989 by
Wayland (Publishers) Ltd.
61 Western Road, Hove
East Sussex BN3 1JD, England

Editors : Hazel Songhurst and Joan Walters
Designer: Kudos Services

**British Library Cataloguing in
Publication Data**
Roussel, Mike
  Scrap Materials
  1. Activities for children
  I. Title II. Walker, Malcolm S.
  III. Series

ISBN 1-85210-672-7

Typeset by Kudos Editorial and Design Services,
Sussex, England.
**Printed in Italy by G. Canale & C. S.p.A. Turin
and bound in Belgium by Casterman S.A.**

Contents

Introduction   4
Faces and masks   6
People and animals   8
Model buildings   10
Two-storey house   12
A shadow theatre   14
Metal collage   16
Model vehicles   18
Musical instruments   20
Life-size puppets   22
A ferris wheel   24
A merry-go-round   26
Make a book   28
Notes for parents and teachers 30
Books to read   30
Index   32

Introduction

Tools and equipment

These are the main tools to make the projects:
Junior saw
Craft knife and
 metal ruler
Scissors
Hammer
Bradawl or knitting
 needle
Pencil and ruler
Small stapler
PVA glue
 (or specialist glue
 for fabric and
 metal)
Masking tape
Workboard
 60cm x 40cm. Use
 wood, hardboard,
 thick cardboard,
 or even several
 thicknesses of
 newspaper.
Small vice

Scrap is just about anything we throw away. What this book aims to do is to look at some different kinds of household scrap and see how to use it for making all kinds of toys and models. Once you have practised on the projects in the book, you can have fun creating and designing your own models. Here are a few points to help you begin:

1. It is a good idea to collect pictures of things you want to make and look closely at them. What shapes can you see? Do the shapes remind you of any scrap you have seen around the house? Think about what you could use to build different things.
2. Collect various scrap materials, like empty plastic containers, cereal packets, eggboxes, food trays and so on.
3. Pick up a container and look at it carefully. What does it remind you of? Turn it sideways, then upside down. Could it be a lorry, or a house, or does it look like a face or an animal?

The projects in this book are designed to show you how you can use ideas. You do not have to stick exactly to the design of the project, you can add your own ideas and improvements. If you find a project too difficult then move on to an easier one, or experiment with the idea and see if you can make something different.

Materials

Plastic containers
Detergent bottles, squash bottles, thoroughly rinced shampoo bottles, ice-cream containers, yoghurt pots, margarine tubs, plastic plates, food trays.

Cardboard packaging
Cereal boxes, all kinds of food packets and boxes, shoe boxes, eggboxes, cardboard plates, cups and tubes.

Polystyrene
Polystyrene dishes, trays, eggboxes, tiles, packaging shapes (shops receive goods packed in them, so do schools).

Warning
Do not use empty bleach containers, aerosol cans or any container with a *"Keep away from children "* warning.

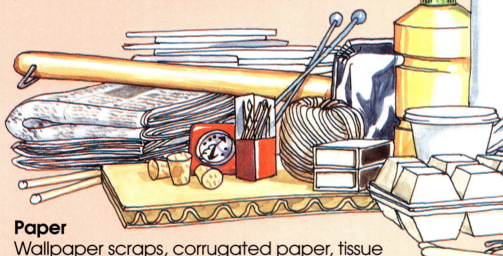

Paper
Wallpaper scraps, corrugated paper, tissue paper, newspapers and magazines.

Odds and ends
Fabric scraps, knitted yarns, cotton wool, paper clips, corks, wooden lolly sticks, broom handles, dowel rods, buttons, cocktail sticks, straws, metal washers, cellophane, old clock workings, pipe-cleaners, screw-hooks and eyes, elastic string, matchboxes, clothes pegs, old clothes.

Sort your scrap into different boxes. Smaller items can be kept in tins, old jars, etc.

Faces and masks

You will need

- 1 polystyrene dish or tray
- 3 buttons
- Coloured fur-fabric scraps
- Cotton wool or strands of wool
- 6 polystyrene packing shapes (or tile you can cut up)
- PVA glue
- Bradawl or knitting needle
- Paint or felt-tips
- Elastic or string
- Reference pictures for ideas

It is easy to make faces and masks from polystyrene food trays. Cardboard plates are just as good.

1. Glue on buttons for eyes, polystyrene shapes for eyebrows, lips and ears. Paint or draw on a nose or glue on a large button or if you like, use a cork or section of eggbox.

2. For hair, glue on fur fabric, cotton wool or knot eight to ten strands of wool together and glue the knot on to the tray.

3. To make a mask, push two holes through on either side and thread string, wool or elastic through to hold it on. You could make holes for the eyes, nose and mouth as well.

You will need

- 1 cereal box
- Textured wallpaper
- 2 coloured pipe-cleaners
- Cotton wool
- 1 cork
- Cardboard eggbox
- Fur-fabric scraps
- Small paper clips
- Junior saw
- PVA glue
- Bradawl or knitting needle

Cereal box mask

1. Cut a section out of the back of the cereal box for your face to fit into.

2. Glue on textured wallpaper to the front, sides and top of the box. Hold the edges down with paper clips while the glue dries.

3. Saw the cork in half to make a nose. Glue it on. Mark eyeholes and press holes through from the back of the box with a bradawl. Cut two sections from the eggbox, push holes through and glue down on front of box, matching up all the eyeholes. Glue on pipe-cleaner lips and spectacles.

4. Glue on cotton wool for eyebrows and hair and use fur-fabric to make a beard. Make a hole in either side, thread elastic or string through to hold mask on.

More ideas

Make faces or masks with different expressions. Use your family or friends as models. Make scary masks or animal faces. Get together with friends and act a play or story.

People and animals

You will need

- 1 small cardboard tube
- Polystyrene packaging shapes
- 1 eggbox
- Strands of coloured wool
- Scraps of fabric
- PVA or fabric glue
- Paints or felt-pens
- Scissors

A clown

1. Glue a single fabric piece around the cardboard tube but do not cover it completely. Cut out patches of different coloured fabric and stick them on.

2. Cut one section from the eggbox and glue on the top of the tube to make the top of the head.

3. Glue short strands of wool to the back and sides for the hair (leave a bald patch on top and in the front).

4. Glue on polystyrene shapes for the hands, feet and nose and colour them in. Draw in the eyes and mouth.

A furry dog

1. Cut two sections from the polystyrene eggbox, one to fit each end of the cardboard tube. Glue them together.

2. Cut one section from the cardboard eggbox and glue it on to one end to make the nose. Cut a polystyrene shape in half to make two ears. Glue them on to the head.

3. To make the legs, bend two pipe-cleaners in the middle and stick on with masking tape underneath the cardboard tube. Bend the ends to make paws. You can bend the legs so the dog sits or stands.

4. Cut the wool into short strands. Spread glue over the top and sides of the tube and stick on the wool. Colour in nose, eyes and ears.

You will need

- 1 small cardboard tube
- Polystyrene packaging shapes
- 1 polystyrene eggbox
- 1 cardboard eggbox
- 2 pipe-cleaners
- Masking tape
- Strands of wool
- PVA glue
- Scissors
- Felt-pens and paint

Model buildings

You will need

- Box with 4 lift up flaps
- Wooden lolly sticks
- Corrugated paper
- Stiff card
- Eggbox
- PVA glue
- Masking tape
- Scissors
- Pencil and ruler
- Junior saw

This is one idea for making a house that can be used to make different buildings.

1. Open out the 4 box flaps. Make sure the small side flaps are on the outside before fixing the 2 main flaps together with masking tape to make the roof. Trim the side flaps and stick them to the main flaps with masking tape.

2. Measure one side of the roof and cut two pieces of stiff card 2 cm longer and 4 cm wider. Join together with masking tape and glue the card on to the roof.

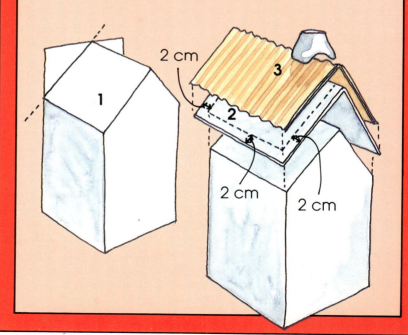

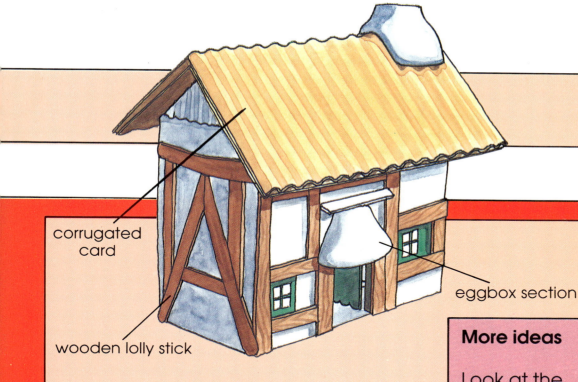

corrugated
card

wooden lolly stick

eggbox section

3. Glue corrugated paper on to the card to make thatch. Cut out eggbox sections for chimneys. Glue them on.

4. Saw the rounded ends off the lolly sticks and glue them to the front of the house to look like timbers.

5. Draw a door and window shapes on the card, cut out and glue them on. Fix a canopy over the door using half an eggbox section.

6. Paint and decorate the house when the glue has dried.

More ideas

Look at the different buildings in your area. Make a model of your own house. Draw on bricks or make roof tiles by overlapping pieces of corrugated paper. Some buildings have flat roofs. Glue on lolly sticks for wooden houses and buildings. Use cellophane for windows. You can make walls textured by spreading on glue and sprinkling with grit or sand.

Two-storey house

You will need

- 2 shoe boxes the same size
- One shoe box lid
- Stiff card
- Wooden lolly sticks
- Scraps for furniture: matchboxes, used matches, polystyrene shapes, eggbox sections, cork-tile scraps.
- Fabric scraps for curtains or carpet
- Cocktail sticks
- Wallpaper scraps
- Cellophane
- PVA glue
- Masking tape
- Scissors, craft knife
- Pencil and ruler
- Paints

1. Cut the door and windows out of the box. Glue on lolly sticks for frames.

2. Measure the width of the box and cut out a piece of stiff card 2 cm longer, for the inside wall. Cut out a doorway and glue on wallpaper.

3. Measure in 1 cm at each end of the wall. Score with a knife and fold. Use glue and masking tape to fix it securely into the box.

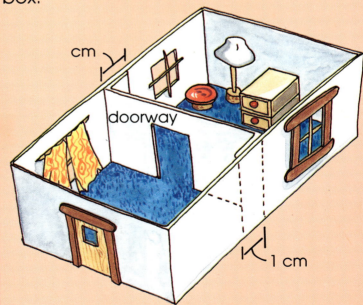

4. Glue on scraps of fabric for carpets, or cork strips or lolly sticks to make a floor. Make curtains from fabric, with cocktail sticks for curtain poles.

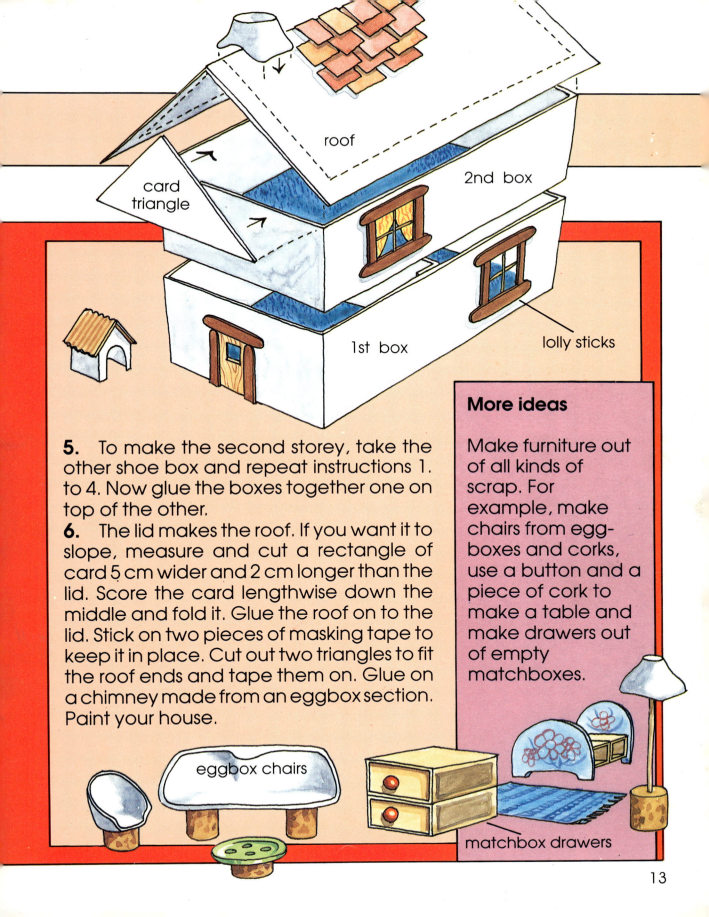

roof

card triangle

2nd box

1st box

lolly sticks

5. To make the second storey, take the other shoe box and repeat instructions 1. to 4. Now glue the boxes together one on top of the other.

6. The lid makes the roof. If you want it to slope, measure and cut a rectangle of card 5 cm wider and 2 cm longer than the lid. Score the card lengthwise down the middle and fold it. Glue the roof on to the lid. Stick on two pieces of masking tape to keep it in place. Cut out two triangles to fit the roof ends and tape them on. Glue on a chimney made from an eggbox section. Paint your house.

More ideas

Make furniture out of all kinds of scrap. For example, make chairs from egg-boxes and corks, use a button and a piece of cork to make a table and make drawers out of empty matchboxes.

eggbox chairs

matchbox drawers

A shadow theatre

You will need

- Large cardboard box (about 50cm x 50 cm x 50 cm)
- Thick tracing paper (about 53 cm x 53 cm x 53 cm)
- Craft knife, scissors
- Thin card
- 25 cm length of dowelling (for holding puppets)
- Coloured tissue paper
- PVA glue, masking tape
- Fabric scraps
- Corrugated card
- Cocktail sticks
- Pencil, ruler
- Wallpaper scraps
- Paints, felt-pens
- Anglepoise lamp

You may need adult help with part of this project.

1. Cut out the front of the theatre with a craft knife or scissors. Ask an adult to do this.

2. Cut about 34 cm long and 2 cm wide strip down the sides and along the top of the box. Make it 3 cm in from the edges.

3. Fix the tracing paper to the front with masking tape.

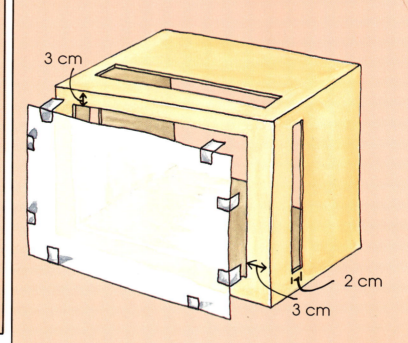

4. Use fabric for curtains (there is no need for the curtains to pull). Glue on to the box.

5. Decorate the top and sides of the box with wallpaper scraps or paint. Draw on designs with felt-pens.

6. Make the puppets. Draw a shape on to card and cut it out. Stick a small piece of corrugated card on to the back of the puppet so the grooves run across. Tape a cocktail stick on to one end of a length of dowelling. The cocktail stick will fit into the grooves in the corrugated card.

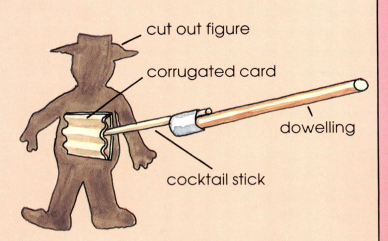

cut out figure

corrugated card

dowelling

cocktail stick

7. Position the anglepoise lamp behind the theatre. Adjust it so the light does not shine directly into the back.

Scenery

Cut out card shapes of houses, ships, rocks, etc. Stick coloured tissue paper over cut out windows. The colour will show up when you light the theatre. Slip the scenery in through the back, between the front edge and the tracing paper.

Metal collage

You will need

- Clock parts
- Polystyrene tile
- Twigs
- Pipe-cleaners
- Fabric scraps
- Feathers

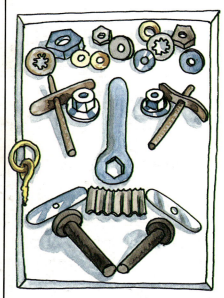

Collect together all kinds of metal scraps such as old nuts, bolts, springs, safety pins, paper clips (you can easily unbend these if you want), wire, old screws, chains, etc. Look hard at the shapes and think about the pictures you could make: cars, people, faces, landscapes, animals. Use all kinds of scrap materials together with metal in your collages - string, elastic bands, eggbox sections, matchboxes, pipe-cleaners, fabric, wallpaper scraps, foil, used matches and anything else that may be useful. A polystyrene tile makes a good base for metal collages - you can press the pieces down into it. You can use it as a base for 3-D models too. If you decide to glue metal to metal, it is best to use specialist glue.

Bird collage

This idea uses parts of an old clock. You can probably find one in a jumble sale or charity shop.

1. Spread out the metal shapes. Arrange your picture as you want it before glueing the pieces down.
2. Spread glue along the twigs and press them down into the polystyrene. Cut out leaves from fabric scraps and glue on.
3. Use the spring for the bird's body, the cogs for head and eye, two hands for the beak, the third hand for the leg and the winder for the tail. Spread glue on each piece and press it down in place on the polystyrene.
4. Glue on feathers for wings. Bend the pipe-cleaner into a worm and glue it in place.

More ideas

Make a picture of a robot using a variety of metal bits and pieces. Use your imagination and create a collage of the inner workings of a machine, a computer for example.

Model vehicles

You will need

- 2 wooden clothes pegs
- 1 matchbox
- 1 cardboard eggbox
- 3 cocktail sticks
- Wooden lolly sticks
- 3 corks
- PVA glue
- Bradawl or knitting needle
- Scissors
- Junior saw
- Paints or felt-pens

You can build different cars using this idea. Make the chassis the same way but alter the body shape by using different scrap materials.

1. Take the clothes pegs apart and glue the halves together side by side.
2. Glue the two sections together to make the chassis.
3. Glue the cocktail sticks into the small gooves to make axles.

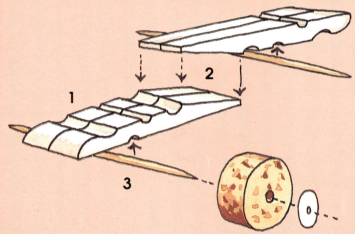

4. Saw four wheels the same size from the corks. Mark the centre of each wheel in pencil and use the bradawl to push a small hole through (remember to press down on to a polystyrene block).

5. Push the wheels on to the axles. Cut out four small circles of card, spread them with glue and push them on to the axles to keep the wheels firm.

6. Cut out sections of eggbox to make the bonnet and seat. Glue them to the chassis. Glue the matchbox on behind the seat.

7. Cut a steering wheel from card or polystyrene and glue it on to a cocktail stick. Put glue on the other end of the stick and push it into the base of the bonnet.

8. Make bumpers by sawing a lolly stick to the width of the car. Stick on circles of eggboxes for lights. Paint your car.

Caterpillar tracks

Use corrugated card to make caterpillar tracks and build a digger, a tank or moon vehicle.

More ideas

Using felt-pens, mark out a roadway on a large sheet of thick card. Put model buildings along the roadsides. Make road signs and traffic signals from card, cocktail sticks, cork, balsa wood, matchboxes.

Musical instruments

You will need

- 2 identical yogurt pots
- Handful of dried rice or beans
- Masking tape
- 4 jam jars
- Jug of water
- 2 lolly sticks or knitting needles
- Small plastic tub (margarine tub will work well)
- 1 large balloon
- Craft knife
- Scissors
- Elastic band

You can make several musical instruments using scrap materials. Here are some suggestions.

Shaker

1. Half fill a yogurt pot with a handful of dried rice or beans.
2. Put the other yogurt pot over the first one and fix it on with masking tape.
3. Shake it to make a pleasing noise.

Xylophone

1. Line up four empty jars.
2. Take a jug of water and fill the first jar. Add less to each of the other jars.
3. Lightly tap each jar in turn with a lolly stick or a knitting needle and listen to the note it makes. You can change the notes by changing the amount of water in the jars.

More ideas

Look around for scrap to make other instruments you can bang, scrape, tap, shake or blow.

Drums

1. Cut a hole in the bottom of a margarine tub using a craft knife.
2. Blow up the balloon as big as you can without bursting it! This will stretch the rubber and make it easier to work with. Split the balloon down one side with scisssors.
3. Stretch the balloon tightly over the top of the carton and secure with an elastic band.
4. Use a lolly stick to beat your drum.

balloon

elastic band

cut

Life-size puppets

You will need

- 1 large plastic bottle with handle (squash bottle)
- 1 broom handle
- 1 wire coat-hanger
- Junior saw
- Scraps of fur-fabric or wool
- 1 cardboard eggbox
- 1 pipe-cleaner
- Carpet tacks and hammer
- PVA glue, masking tape
- Dowel, 50 cm long
- Card
- Stapler
- Old clothes: shirt, jumper, dress or coat, scarf, hat

You may need adult help with this project.

1. Push the broom handle up inside the neck of the plastic bottle. Pad the bottle with a cardboard tube or newspaper for a good fit. Hammer the tacks in through the bottle neck and into the broom.

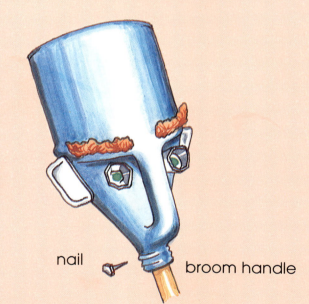

nail   broom handle

2. Cut out eggbox sections to make eyes and ears. (The bottle handle makes the nose.) Glue these on and colour in the eyes. Stick on fur-fabric or wool eyebrows and hair. Make the mouth from the pipe-cleaner and glue it on.

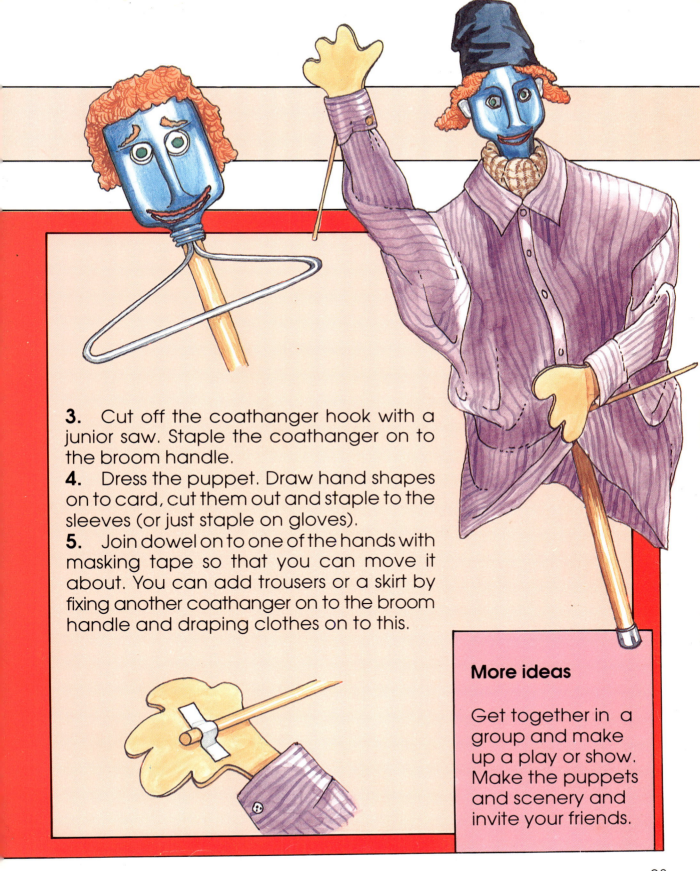

3. Cut off the coathanger hook with a junior saw. Staple the coathanger on to the broom handle.

4. Dress the puppet. Draw hand shapes on to card, cut them out and staple to the sleeves (or just staple on gloves).

5. Join dowel on to one of the hands with masking tape so that you can move it about. You can add trousers or a skirt by fixing another coathanger on to the broom handle and draping clothes on to this.

More ideas

Get together in a group and make up a play or show. Make the puppets and scenery and invite your friends.

A ferris wheel

You will need

- 1 length of wood (38 cm x 8 cm)
- 2 metal coat-hangers
- 32 lolly sticks
- Card
- 2 wooden cotton reels (standard size hole easily takes 5 mm dowel)
- Used matchsticks
- 8 eggbox sections
- Strong thread and needle
- 1 length of dowel: 8 cm long x 5 mm wide
- PVA glue
- Stapler
- Pencil, ruler
- Bradawl or knitting needle
- Craft knife

1. Draw two circles 8 cm in diameter on to card.

2. Cut out the circles and make a hole in the centre of each large enough to take the dowel.

3. Put the cotton reel over the hole on each circle (making sure the holes line up) and draw round.

4. With pencil and ruler, divide each circle into two, then four, then eight sections. Glue on eight lolly sticks along the lines you have drawn, round the small circle.

5. When dry, glue eight more lolly sticks on to each circle, to make the edges. Glue on the first four, leaving spaces in between. When they are dry, glue on the other four.

6. Turn one card over and glue the cotton reel over the central hole. Wait for the glue to dry before glueing the second circle on top.

7. Measure the distance between the lolly sticks and cut eight matchsticks slightly longer. This will make sure they fit tightly. Glue the matchsticks in place.

8. Bend the coat hanger hooks round into circles the right size for the dowel to run smoothly through.

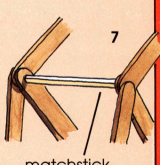

7

matchstick

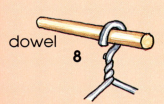

dowel

8

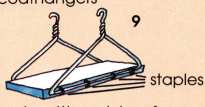

coathangers

9

staples

thread

12

eggbox seat

9. Staple the hangers on to either side of the wood base. Make sure they are the same height. Push the dowel through the wheel.

10. On to card, draw round the second cotton reel. Cut out four circles. Make a hole in the centre of each to take the dowel.

11. Push two of the circles on to the dowel on either side of the wheel. Fit the ferris wheel in between the coathangers. Fit the other two card circles on either side.

12. Push needle and thread through one side of eggbox seat. Secure with a knot. Loop thread over and round a matchstick. Take it down through the other hole. Adjust length of thread, making sure seat clears the base when wheel turns. Secure the thread with a knot. Fix on the other seats.

13. Decorate the ferris wheel with colours and patterns. Visit a real fair or look in books for ideas.

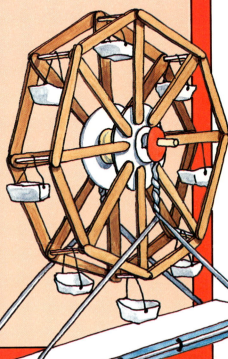

A merry-go-round

You will need

- 1 round cardboard cheesebox
- 1 bottle cork
- 1 round plastic lid about 8 cm across
- 9 cocktail sticks
- 2 metal washers
- Wallpaper scraps
- Polystyrene packaging shapes
- PVA glue
- Scissors, pencil, ruler
- Junior saw
- Bradawl or knitting needle

1. Draw round cheesebox top on to wallpaper. Put this to one side.

2. Cut the cork in two. Glue half on to centre of plastic lid. Dip cocktail stick in glue and push it into the cork. Place a washer over the top.

3. Put the top on the cheesebox, turn it over and with pencil and ruler, divide box into eight. Push eight holes right through all around the edge and one through the centre.

2   3

4. Separate cheesebox. Trim sharp points off the cocktail sticks and glue them into the base.

5. Fit the base over cocktail stick in cork. Put on the second washer. Push second cork half down on to stick.

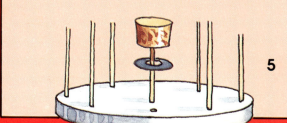

5

6. Push the cheesebox top down over sticks so that they protrude through the top. A spot of glue at each hole will hold them firmly.

7. Cut out the circle of wallpaper. Cut an upside-down V from edge to centre. Glue the cut edges together to make the domed canopy. Glue this on inside the circle of sticks.

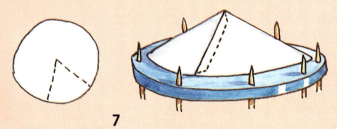

8. Cut out eight wallpaper triangles to make flags and glue them on the cocktail sticks. Make fairground horses, seats or cars from polystyrene shapes and glue on. Paint and decorate the merry-go-round.

More ideas

Think of other fairground rides or stalls you could make out of all kinds of materials. A coconut shy is easy, using a polystyrene block, plastic mesh, cocktail sticks and plasticine.

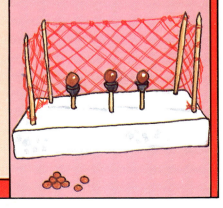

Make a book

You will need

- Wide masking tape (5 cm)
- Wallpaper scraps
- PVA glue
- Large blunt needle (e.g. embroidery needle)
- 2 pieces stiff card each 20 cm x 12 cm
- 10 sheets A4 paper
- Scissors
- Craft knife
- Bradawl or knitting needle

1. On each piece of card, measure in 2 cm from one edge and draw a line down.
2. Cut 24 cm length of masking tape. Stick it along the line on one piece of card. Press the other edge of the masking tape carefully along the line on the second card. Turn the ends of the masking tape over and press down. Turn the whole thing over and fill in the centre with another piece of masking tape.

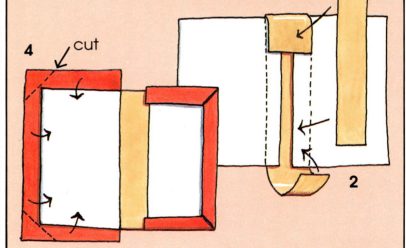

3. Cut out two rectangles of wallpaper, each 26 cm x 15 cm. Glue them down on to the card. Position the wallpaper carefully up to the edge of the masking tape, so there is an even overlap at top and bottom.
4. Turn the book over. Cut off the corners and fold the extra wallpaper over and glue it down.

5. Fold the A4 sheets in half. Measure 12 cm along from the fold and draw a line down. With craft knife or scissors , cut along this line.

6. Measure 19 cm down from the top edge and draw a line across. Cut along this line.

7. Open out the paper. Measure down the fold to find the centre and mark it. Push a hole through the centre and make two more holes, one 4 cm above and one 4 cm below the centre.

8. Thread the needle with about 30 cm of thread and knot the end.

9. Push the needle and thread down through the centre hole and up through the top hole, then back through the centre hole. Come back up through the bottom hole and back through the centre hole. Knot the thread securely at the back, making sure it is tight enough to keep the pages firmly together.

10. Paste the outer pages down on to the inside covers. Put card in between the cover and the pages to stop the pages sticking together while the paste dries. Close the book and put a weight on top. Leave for several hours.

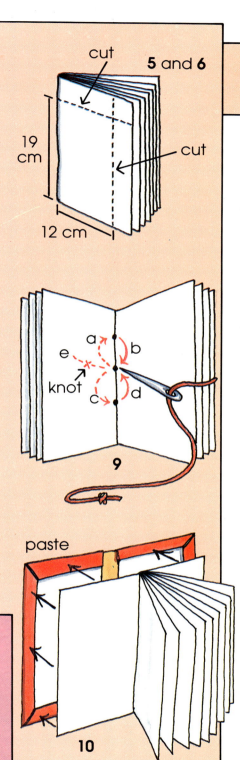

More ideas

Make your own folders for school projects.
Use cloth instead of wallpaper for the cover. Make a plain cover and then decorate it with felt-pens, cut-out pictures, or printed design. If you use cloth for the cover, you need fabric glue to stick it.

Notes for parents and teachers

Books to read

Children and adults can gain many more ideas for building with scrap materials from the following books.

THE KNOWHOW BOOK OF ACTION TOYS by Heather Amery (Usborne, 1975).

THE KNOWHOW BOOK OF ACTION GAMES by Anne Civardi (Usborne, 1975).

PUPPETS (*Fresh Start series*) by Lyndie Wright (Franklin Watts, 1988).

PRITT CRAFT BOOK (Knight, 1985).

All children, from pre-school age onwards, enjoy using their hands and their imagination in creative activity. Making things from scrap is inexpensive and fun and an ideal home-based activity. Interest and support from parents is an essential ingredient, from encouraging a collection of useful scrap materials to discussing ideas and giving a hand with more ambitious projects.

At school, making from scrap materials is a long-established activity. It is a good idea to sort different scrap into storage boxes and encourage children to choose their own materials. It is also helpful to cut up some materials into different shapes to help stimulate ideas. Some children may not be aware of the possibilities and this may help them. Others will come up with ideas that had not occurred to their teacher.

Group work can be particularly worthwhile especially in problem-solving activities, where discussion and interaction between the children results in a solution to a problem.

Making things from scrap can, of course be linked with topic work. Many of the basic projects in this book can be adapted to topics across the curriculum.

Lifesize creations can be particularly inspiring as part of class projects. Building an environment (such as a spaceship cabin, or a Victorian kitchen) that children can move around in, or populate with puppets, will make a positive atmosphere to learning. There is something special and satisfying to a child about playing, or working in an environment which he or she helped create.

Safety

Handle all tools sensibly. If in doubt, ask an adult. Some projects may need adult help - do not try to do them alone.

Junior saw
Hold the piece you are cutting firmly (against a bench hook or in a small vice).

Craft knife
Use the craft knife only when you cannot use scissors. If cutting along a line, cut against a metal ruler. Cut on a firm surface like the workboard. Do not press too hard and cut a section at a time. If trimming cork or wood, cut away from yourself.

Bradawl
To make a hole in something, it is a good idea to use a polystyrene block (two old tiles stuck together) as your workboard so that the bradawl pushes down on to it and does not injure you or the table. A knitting needle is just as good. Use different thicknesses for different sized holes.

Be a tidy worker. Clean all tools and brushes and put everything away when you have finished.

SCRAP MATERIALS

Index

caterpillar tracks 19
collecting scrap 4
colouring:
  felt-pens 6, 8, 9, 14,
  18, 19
  paints 6, 8, 12, 13,
  14, 18, 19, 27

decoration 11, 13,
  15, 25, 27

equipment 4-5

furniture 13

materials 5
metal scraps 16-17

old clothes 22-23

pictures 16-17
plasticine 27
projects:
  coconut shy 27
  faces and masks
  6-7
  make a book
  28-29
  merry-go-round
  26-27

metal collage
16-17
model building
10-11
model vehicle
18-19
musical instruments
20-21
people and
animals 8-9
puppets 15, 22-23
road signs 19
scenery 15
shadow theatre
14-15
traffic signals 19
two-storey house
12-13

safety 5, 31

tools 4-5